WITH ONE WHITE WING

ELIZABETH SPIRES

WITH ONE WHITE WING

J 811
SPI

PUZZLES
IN
POEMS AND PICTURES

ILLUSTRATED BY ERIK BLEGVAD

MARGARET K. McELDERRY BOOKS

Margaret K. McElderry Books
An imprint of Simon & Schuster Children's Publishing Division
1230 Avenue of the Americas
New York, New York 10020

Designed by Nancy Williams
The text of this book is set in Baskerville.
The illustrations were done in watercolor.
Printed in Hong Kong by South China Printing Company (1988) Ltd.
Printed on recycled paper

10 9 8 7 6 5 4 3   2 1

Library of Congress Cataloging-in-Publication Data
Spires, Elizabeth.
With one white wing : puzzles in poems and pictures / by Elizabeth Spires ; illustrations by Erik Blegvad.
p.   cm.
ISBN 0-689-50622-8
1. Children's poetry.   2. Puzzles—Juvenile literature.   3. Riddles, Juvenile.
[1. Riddles.   2. Picture puzzles.   3. American poetry.]
I. Blegvad, Erik, ill.   II. Title.
PN6109.97.S67   1995
811'.54—dc20   94-12927
SUMMARY: A collection of twenty-six puzzles, illustrated in full color, with verbal and
pictorial hints, ranging in answer from a bumblebee to a swimming pool.

For Celia
—E. S.

Two hands hold me.
Two feet avoid me.

Jump!
Or I'll trip you up.

jump rope

8

Zzzzzzzzzzzzzzzzzzzzzzzzzzzzzzzzzzzzzz!
I have ten thousand teeth
but I never go to the dentist.

zipper.

I have five arms but no head.
I sleep in a water bed.
I never see what I am named after.

starfish

If you see one of us,
you'll see the other.
We're opposites, though,
like a sister and brother.
At breakfast, lunch, and dinner,
we get all shook up.

salt and pepper shakers

Our queen lives in a castle
without any king.
She has a sweet tooth.
She loves sweet sticky things.

So we, her loyal army,
march in a long black line
through the countryside
and bring back what we can find—

cake crumbs, sweetmeats, pie!

ants

I am white and round,
wrapped in the layers
of a papery gown.
When I'm cut apart,
people cry over me.

onion

Spring, summer, fall, winter,
I like to dress and undress.
I have black bones
and pale green flesh.

tree

All day I lie in bed on the lawn,
attracting attention, basking in the sun.

I have two lips, two lips, two lips,
but I can't kiss, can't kiss, can't kiss.

tulip

I have one eye.
If you ask me how I feel,
I'll say, "So-so."

needle

I'm tall and thin.
I stand at attention
in the kitchen
with all my friends.

At dinner, hands throw us
into a boiling pot.
We go limp with shock
and are quickly eaten up.

spaghetti

I bumble along like a blimp,
awkwardly bumping into things.
I wear a black and yellow sweater
in the hottest summer weather.
Don't touch me. Don't interfere.
I have a terrible temper.

bumblebee

If you smile at me,
I'll smile back.
If you frown,
I'll do the same.
When you leave I get bored
and pretend I'm a room.

mirror

I can count to 12,
but I don't know my ABCs.
I have a face,
and two hands, sometimes three.
I'm always telling people
what to do next.

clock

I'm red, then green,
then red, then green.
I can't seem
to stop changing.

Stop! No, go!
No, stop!
Do what I say
or you'll be sorry!

traffic light

I weigh less than a feather
but you can't pick me up.
I can dance but I can't sing.
Without you, I am nothing.

shadow

I'm from a big family,
a dozen usually.
We were born to be
cracked and beaten,
flipped over and eaten.
Life is rough but
we're hardboiled about it.

egg

Do you like to hide in dark places?
(I do.)

Do you like to surprise people?
(I do.)

If I ask you nicely,
will you let me out of this box?

BOO!

jack-in-the-box

Bzzzzzz!
I'm not a bee, a bee
would make a dozen of me.

Bzzzzzz!
At night I sing in your ear, sing
a song you don't want to hear.

Bzzzzzz!
I'm a kamikaze.
My bite is worse than my buzz.

mosquito

Once I had a cheerful face,
round and yellow as the sun.
Those days are over,
those days are gone.

Overnight my hair
and whiskers turned white.
The next windy day
will blow me away.

dandelion

Outside all winter
I never shiver.

I never burn or freeze
but adjust by degrees
to spring and fall.

But hot summer days
go to my head
and I see red!

thermometer

Feathered, I fly
with help from you.
You always bend.
I'm straight and true.

Out of many,
I was chosen.
I quiver
at the honor.

arrow

With one white wing,
I fly over the water.
Puffed with pride,
I race the wind
(we always tie),
but if the wind dies,
so do I.

sailboat

I climb a thin string
that hangs in the air,
then slide back down
without getting anywhere.

I have my ups and downs
but doesn't everyone?

yo-yo

My life is as long
as an evening.
The older I am,
the shorter I am
until I am nothing.

candle

I can be empty or full
(without ever eating).
I can be warm or cold
(without ever feeling).
I can be deep or shallow
(without ever thinking).
I can watch you sink
(without ever blinking).
I'm calmest when you leave me alone.

swimming pool

My life is short,
a minute or so.
Look through my round walls
and you'll see a rainbow.

Oh dear! A pin!
Pop! I'm gone.

soap bubble